America & Liberia

A Mother/Stepchild Relationship Betrayed

By

Dr. J. Mamadee Ghorpu-Dolo Woah-Tee, Sr.

authorHOUSE

1663 LIBERTY DRIVE, SUITE 200
BLOOMINGTON, INDIANA 47403
(800) 839-8640
www.authorhouse.com

First published by AuthorHouse 12/07/04

ISBN: 1-4184-3141-9 (e)
ISBN: 1-4184-3140-0 (sc)

Printed in the United States of America
Bloomington, Indiana

This book is printed on acid-free paper.

ABOUT THE AUTHOR

The author, J. Mamadee Ghorpu-Dolo Woah-Tee, Sr., is the son of the late Clan Chief Daiwor Togbah Woah-Tee and Nangba Nanlon of Gbaomu, Jorpole Clan, Bong County, Liberia. J. Mamadee Woah-Tee, Sr. is an Educational Administrator.

J. Mamadee is married to Cecelia Lorpu Paye-Woah-Tee and they are blessed with five children(Daiwor Togbah Woah-Tee, II, (age 29), Josephine Ndeimei Woah-Tee, (27), Ghorpu, (22), Nyeinpu(17), J. Mamadee Ghorpu-Dolo Woah-Tee, Jr.(12), and a grandson, Daiwor Togbah Woah-Tee, III (7).

J. Mamadee, Sr. obtained his elementary and Junior High School education from the William V.S. Tubman Elementary and Junior High School, Gbarnga Methodist Mission in 1963. He matriculated to the Dolokelen Gboveh Jr. & Senior High School in 1964. He graduated from Gboveh in 1967. He entered the University of Liberia in 1968 and graduated in 1972 as an education major. J. Mamadee entered the school of Graduate Studies, Morgan State University, Baltimore, Maryland, U.S.A in August of 1978 and in the summer of 1979, he completed the requirements of his Masters degree in Educational Administration and Supervision. In May of 1980, he was awarded the degree. Since the Government of Liberia gave him two years to do his Masters and he did it in one year, he decided to go for a second Masters but this time in the area of Elementary and Middle School Curriculum. He began this program of studies in August of 1979 and also completed its requirements in the summer of 1980. In May, 1981, he was awarded the degree. In August, 1991, J. Mamadee, Sr. earned his terminal degree, Doctor of Philosophy, in Education, Policy, Planning and Administration from the University of Maryland, College Park, Maryland, U.S.A.

TEACHING and ADMINISTRATIVE EXPERIENCE:

From 1973 to 1975, J. Mamadee, Sr. taught 7th, 8th and 9th grade Social Studies at the Dolokelen Gboveh Junior and Senior High School, Gbarnga, Bong County. From July 1975 to August 1978, he served as the first Principal of the new Gboveh Multilateral

High School, Gbarnga, Bong County. During the same years(1975-1978), he served as Principal of the Peoples High School that was established for working adults/youths of the county during the evening; up to 10:P.M. Monday through Friday of each week. J. Mamadee currently serves as TEACHER-AMBASSADOR for the Baltimore-Gbarnga Sister Cities relationship that was established in 1971.

ORGANIZATIONS:

1. Served as first President, the Dolokelen Gboveh Senior High School Student Government

2. Served as President, Bong Varsity Students Association, University of Liberia;

3. Served as President, the Union of Liberian Associations in the Americas(ULAA);

4. First African to served as President, All Saint Lutheran Church Council, Baltimore, Maryland;

5. Served as Co-Chairman, Gbarnga-Baltimore Sister Cities Committee, U.S.A.;

6. Served as the President of the Bong County Teachers Association;

7. Served as President of the Bong County High School Principals Association;

8. Serves as Chairman, Board of Directors, Gboveh Alumni Association in the Americas

9. Serves as President, Bong County, Liberia/Maryland, U.S.A. Educational/Cultural Foundation, Inc;

10. Developed the Gaimei N.N. Woah-Tee Neighborhood Center, Baltimore, Maryland, U.S.A.

11. Served as Administrative Assistant to the Dean of Continuing Education, Morgan State University

THE AUTHOR'S CONCEPT OF LEADERSHIP

Leadership is an invisible strand

as mysterious as it is powerful.

It pulls and it bonds.

It is a catalyst that creates unity out of disorder.

Yet, it defies definition.

No combination of talents can guarantee it.

No process of training can create it where the spark does not exist.

The qualities of leadership are universal.

They are found in the poor and the rich,

the humble and the proud,

the common man, and the brilliant thinker,

they are qualities that suggest paradox rather than pattern.

But wherever they are found

leadership makes things happen.

The most precious and intangible quality of leadership is trust—

the confidence that the one who leads will act in the best interest of

those who follow—

the assurance that he will serve the group without sacrificing the

rights of the individual.

Leadership's imperative is a "sense of rightness"—

knowing when to advance and when to pause.

When to criticize and when to praise,

how to encourage others to excel.

From the leader's reserves of energy and optimism,

his followers draw strength.

In his determination and self confidence, they find inspiration.

In its highest sense, leadership is integrity.

This command by conscience asserts itself more by commitment

and example than by directive.

Integrity recognizes external obligation, but it heeds

the quiet voice within, rather than the clamor without.

Summary

The individuals who I have chosen to dedicate this document to, were ones who fit the descriptions given earlier of what leadership is all about. These very important individuals who helped to make me what I am today are the late President William Richard Tolbert, Jr of Liberia, Mr. J. Kolleh Yorwatei, former Superintendent, Bong County, Liberia, the late Paramount Chief Dolokelen Paye, Panta Chiefdom, Bong County, Liberia and the late Clan Chief Daiwor Togbah Woah-Tee, my father, Jorpole Clan, Bong County, Liberia.

Two of the honorees, Tolbert and Yorwatei, can be identified with the Western World because of the levels of formal education. Chiefs Paye and Woah-Tee had no formal education, but were traditional leaders for their tribal settings. The leadership that these individuals provided for their constituents is a classic example of a Godly visionary leadership. They served their constituents with one thing in mind-that leaders are mere servants. While each had his own weaknesses, they made things happen on the whole; in the interest of the governed and the nation. They could be trusted and were men of with integrity.

All objectives and truth loving Liberians will agree that the late President William R. Tolbert, Jr. was a true leader with a unique sense of direction for Liberia and perhaps the most progressive leader in the history of Liberia. President Tolbert's sense of Nationalism and vision for the country were the highest since independence. His regard for fair play in Government, the strict application of rules regardless of who you are, determination and honesty for the total upholding, protection and defense of the Constitution of Liberia were among the priorities of his Administration. Unlike his predecessor, Tolbert refused to usurp the powers of the other branches of the Liberian Government.

"I will not lead a nation whose citizens' minds I do not know" said Tolbert in August of 1971, few weeks after his ascendancy to the Presidency of Liberia. In order to fulfill his promise, he unlocked the door on fundamental freedoms theretofore locked in the closets of the Executive Mansion, including freedoms of expression and a free press. Cognizant of the oath of office he took, Tolbert fairly and honestly performed those constitutional duties that were required of him no matter who they affected. Among the first of several actions that Tolbert took early in his Administration was to bring to justice those who had committed heinous crimes against the indigenous population and were allowed to enjoy their freedom under a corrupted so-called "Portage System" designed by Americo-Liberian elites, fostered and enforced by the prior Administration of William V.S. Tubman. True, Tolbert himself participated in and upheld the practice prior to his ascendancy to the Presidency, but only out of fear of retaliation from Tubman. Treason, as it was called, was punishable by indefinite incarceration and/or execution.

The evils of the Portage System, including forced enslavement and servitude by the America-Liberians- led government, were brought to an end early in the Tolbert Administration through his sweeping government reforms that brought PEACE of MINDS to the tribal people of Bong County(Kpelle tribe), Lofa County(Lorma, Gissi, Gbarne, etc. tribes), Nimba County(Gio and Mano tribes) and Grand Gedeh County(the Khran tribe). Among them was the establishment of a system akin to a "civil service" whereby tribal chiefs were put on salaries; thus putting an end to the bribery and corruption of the past and reform of the government's tax policies to ensure fairness and equity for all Liberians.

The second man I honor here is Mr. J. Kolleh Yorwatei, for his tireless work to solve the problems of the poor indigenous of his territory. Former Superintendent of Bong County and private secretary to the late Tolbert during his term as Vice President of Liberia, Yorwatei was successful in putting an end to local corruption and the practice of illegal collections from uneducated tribal people and the encroachment of their lands. He is recognized for his commitment to local development and emphasis on education as well.

The next Honoree I commend for his defense of his people against the corrupt elite is the late Paramount Chief Dolokelen Paye of Panta Chiefdom, Bong County, Liberia. The late Paramount, unlike his successors, was a caring, loving and one of the most powerful chiefs of his time. He often challenged the District and County leaders in their attempts to take advantage of his tribal people. He stressed education as the primary means of lifting up his people and worked to get the government to build an elementary and Junior High School in Fokweleh, his Chiefdom's headquarters.

Finally, I honor the late Clan Chief Daiwor Togbah Woah-Tee, my father for the type of leadership he provided for the people of his "Quarter," Town and Clan. He deserves credit for the Godly visionary leadership he provided for the people of his Town and the Jorpool Clan, Bong County. He served as a traditional leader on three levels, the first being Quarter Chief, then Town Chief and lastly, Clan Chief. He was a leader with integrity whom people trusted.

Chief Woah-Tee vigorously opposed the Portage System and the inhumane and suppressive treatment of his people by the America-Liberian led government. I owe a deep debt of gratitude to him for having made it possible for my educational achievement and the path down which I was led in my early youth.

He worked tirelessly in advancing the values of an education system and the benefits of a formal education. As Town Chief of Gbaomu, Bong County, he built an elementary school that benefited the children of his town and surrounding towns in 1970. The school was ultimately turned over to the Ministry of Education which supported it through the assignment of teachers.

He understood the power of the marketplace and among his many projects, built a Farm-to-Market road which served to enhance his popularity among his people, officials of the Bong County Government and eventually, led to his election in 1975 as Clan Chief of Jorpool Clan in a landslide. Chief Woah-Tee retired at the completion of his term and traveled to Baltimore, Maryland, U.S.A. to spent time with his children. Three years later, he passed away. His body was returned to his homeland where he was laid to rest with honors. "Old man Woah-Tee," as he was commonly called by his people as well as county officials, was honored by many dignitaries, including former Mayor Kurt L. Schmoke of Baltimore City, some members of Congress from the State of Maryland, U.S.A., a United States Senator(Honorable Barbara A. Mikulski), the Board of Education, Baltimore City Public School System and the Liberian Association of Maryland.

In addition to the men I honor here today, I want to make a note of special thanks to Mr. Charles Varney Dormeyan, Sr. for the important role he played in the political and infrastructure development of Bong County, Liberia. He worked hard to protect the rights of the poor, uneducated tribal people of the County against local corruption in his twenty five or more years in public life as Administrative Assistant to each of the five Superintendents who served as direct Representative of Presidents Tubman and Tolbert respectively and later, Development Superintendent of Bong County, Liberia.

Table of Contents

I. Introduction

It has been said that Americans will do anything for Latin America but read about it. The same might be said even more strongly of Americans and Africa. Individual dramatic events may capture the public imagination from time to time. Sometimes these events offer an image of hope, such as the release of Nelson Mandela and the fall of apartheid in South Africa. More often they present an image of horror and despair, such as the nearly continent-wide AIDS crisis, or the brutal civil war in Ruwanda that left scores dead and recent French intervention in the Ivory Coast.

Apart from these individual events, however, Americans generally have little consciousness of Africa. Even African-Americans often have little overall knowledge of their ancestors' homeland. Most Americans conceptualize the continent of Africa as a country. Probably few Americans could find the Ivory Coast on a map. If they did, they would find that one of its neighbors is Liberia, and they might hazily recall having read that Liberia was founded in the 19th century by freed slaves from the United States.

In fact, Liberia was, perhaps unofficially, America's first overseas colony, founded in 1822 by the American Colonization Society, which ruled it until it gained Independence in 1847 –

1

peacefully, but on the initiative of the Liberian settlers rather than by grant (Liebenow, 1987, pp. 16-17). Between 1822 and 1904, some 20,000 African-Americans emigrated to Liberia, most in the early decades, but some 4000 in the decades after the American Civil War.

Strong ties of identity and culture remained between the two countries even after immigration trailed off. For over a century up till 1980, Liberia was governed by the True Whig Party. Its name derived from the 19th century American political party. The True Whig Party was controlled and run by the freed American slaves who immigrated to Liberia. The Americo-Liberians, as the settlers' descendants are called, continued to identify strongly with the United States – only to often discover, to their dismay and to the disadvantage of indigenous Liberians, that Americans were scarcely aware of them, or of Liberia itself.

The American colonial origin of Liberia also left its mark in the form of a social contradiction that dominated 20th-century Liberia, and still deeply marks Liberian society. The Americo-Liberians were of African ancestry, but they did not think of themselves as Africans. Nor did they regard the indigenous Africans of Liberia as their fellow-countrymen. They proudly adopted the declaration that "The Love of Liberty Brought Us Here" as Liberia's national motto. They offered no liberty to the indigenous majority of Liberians. Not until 1904 were the indigenous people even admitted to citizenship, which remained nominal for decades more.

Only after 1944 did efforts begin to forge a unified Liberian identity. Even then, Liberia remained essentially a colonialist society until 1980 when the first violent and bloody coup took place. Since 1980, Liberia has struggled with coups, rigged elections, dictatorship, and brutal civil war. The seeds of this strife – as elsewhere in Africa – were planted in the colonial era.

The remainder of this document will examine how the colonial experience shaped modern Liberia, and the persisting effects of Liberia's unwanted-stepchild relationship with the nation that founded it. My examination will proceed along a threefold path: the origins and development of Liberia, the relationship between the Americo-Liberian elites and the indigenous majority, and Liberia's relationship with the United States.

II. Historical Background of Liberia

Black Slavery in America

The African slave trade was integral to the English presence in the New World long before the first successful English colony in North American was established at Jamestown in Virginia in 1607. The Spanish had begun importing African slaves to their colonies early in the 16th century. In the 1560s, English seamen like John Hawkins and Francis Drake began to sail to the Caribbean, originally as smugglers to the Spanish colonies.

The goods they smuggled were slaves bought or kidnapped along the western Atlantic coast lines of Africa. Queen Elizabeth I of England was a silent partner in these smuggling expeditions, chartering royal warships to the smugglers. Only after the third of such slave-trading expeditions was attacked by a Spanish squadron did Hawkins and Drake turn to plundering Spanish galleons instead.

Once English colonies were established in America, slavery soon followed. The sale of "twenty negars" in Jamestown is reported in 1619, the year before the Pilgrims landed at Plymouth Rock. Africans were originally sold as indentured servants – as were many

English – and were freed after a period of years. Soon, however, enslavement of Africans was made permanent.

By the time of the American Revolution, slaves were found in most of the thirteen American colonies. In the northern colonies, these slaves were primarily house servants of the well-to-do, and the total number of slaves in these colonies were small. In the southern colonies, however, plantation slavery had become a mainstay of the economy. Most of the slaves were therefore field hands and African slaves made up a much larger proportion of the population.

Thus, the American Constitution contained the notorious provision that three-fifths(3/5) of "all other Persons" – meaning the slaves – would be counted toward a state's representation in Congress. The Constitution also stipulated that the slave trade could *not* be outlawed before 1808, twenty years after it came into force. The implication, however, was that the salve trade might be forbidden after that date.

In fact, in the early days of the Republic, slavery was widely assumed to be a declining institution. In the North, where the few house slaves were not important to the economy, slavery was increasingly abolished. In the South, where slave labor remained important to the agricultural economy, abolition was not seriously considered. However, the tobacco plantations were in gradual decline, and many people supposed that slavery would eventually die out in the South as well.

The Slavery Question Emerges

From about 1800 on, however, two contrary forces acted to widen the national division over slavery. On the one hand, abolitionist sentiment in the North was on the rise, as people increasingly challenged the perpetuation of slavery in a nation that claimed to be founded on the ideals of Liberty and Equality. This had already been a factor in the abolition of slavery in some northern states.

At the same time, however, Eli Whitney's cotton gin made cotton a highly profitable cash crop in the South. Only a few regions in the South had been suited to growing tobacco, but cotton could be grown far more widely. The booming textile industry in England provided an eager overseas market for cotton. The intensive labor required to grow and pick cotton was regarded as well-suited to plantations worked by gangs of slaves.

Thus, instead of gradually dying out, plantation slavery in the South underwent a revival. In the North, abolitionist sentiment grew stronger in response. The controversy over whether slavery would spread to the new states being formed from Western territories became the central issue in American politics, ultimately setting the stage for the Civil War and the Emancipation Proclamation.

Meanwhile, the question arose in abolitionist circles of what to do about freed slaves – those who had already been freed in the North, a few that were freed from time to time in the South, and the millions who would be freed if slavery was abolished. By modern standards, even many abolitionists had racist attitudes. Many doubted that it was neither desirable nor possible for freed slaves to enter the mainstream of American life.

The Repatriation Option

One alternative option that drew increasing attention as the abolitionist movement grew was repatriation to Africa. The idea of repatriation had a simple logic that was appealing to many abolitionists and others. The slaves had come from Africa in the first place, bought or kidnapped there – and indeed were still coming, also, given that the salve trade had been outlawed, it had not yet been fully suppressed. What, then, could be more natural than to return freed slaves to their homeland?

The idea of repatriation first appeared during the American Revolution – ironically, as a British policy. Sir Henry Clinton, the British Commanding General in the southern colonies, issued what J. Gus Liebenow has described as the first "emancipation proclamation" (1987, p. 12). His order guaranteed the freedom of any slaves who rose up against their rebellious masters. This measure led, in 1787, to the founding of Freetown, in what is now Sierra Leone on the western coast of Africa.

Subsequently, resettlement schemes of various types gained support from many quarters. Among the distinguished names who endorsed it were Thomas Jefferson in 1784, Governor James Monroe in 1801, and the leaders of the majority-black Philadelphia Bethel

Church in 1811. Some of these called for "black states" or territories in North America, proposed locations ranging from Louisiana to the Pacific Northwest (Liebenow, 1987, p. 12).

Gradually, however, repatriation to Africa came to the fore. In 1816, the American Colonization Society was formally established. The motives of its white founders and supporters were oddly varied (Ciment, 1998, p. 34). While some were abolitionists, some of the strongest supporters of the movement were Southern planters and slaves owners. They were particularly eager to see "free persons of color" resettled elsewhere for fear that the presence of free blacks would be an incitement to slaves to demand their own freedom (Liebenow, 1987, p. 13). Removing free blacks, they hoped, would reduce this pressure and make slavery more secure.

Other supporters of the repatriation had quite different motives. For some, it was an opportunity to encourage the spread of Christianity into Africa by establishing enclaves of African-descended Christians. For others, it was an opportunity to spread the ideal of Jeffersonian agrarian democracy by establishing former slaves as free small farmers. The fate of this project will be considered later.

Yet, another motive was to deal with the awkward problem of captives freed from slave ships. The outlawing of the slave trade was accompanied by the establishment of naval patrols off the African coast, tasked with suppressing the slave trade and intercepting slaves. What to do with the captives thus freed, however, was a perplexing problem. The slave trade had extended its tentacles far into the interior of Africa and many captives came from regions where no European had ever been.

Thus, actually sending them home was effectively impossible (and might simply lead to their recapture and return to the slave-trade "pipeline"). Resettlement somewhere in Africa thus seemed a more feasible alternative – the more so since whites tended to regard "Africa" as an undifferentiated mass. Captives freed from slave ships would in fact form an important component of the Liberian colonization, making up about a quarter of the total colonists. The role of this group, who had been sold as slaves but who never reached the Americas, will be discussed later.

Contradictions of Repatriation

The underlying problem with the logic of repatriation was that while the slaves' and former slaves' ancestry was predominantly African, they themselves were not Africans. They were, in present-day usage, African-Americans. Most were generations removed from Africa. A handful of ancestral words and customs might have survived in African-American communities and individual families, but the culture of African-Americans was then what it is now: American culture, as shaped by the black American experience.

Thus, repatriation in any true sense was impossible, save for the relatively few black Americans who were first-generation and still had homes they could return to. For the vast majority, emigrating to Africa would truly be a form of colonization, pioneering in a new and unfamiliar continent to which they had only remote ancestral ties.

Moreover, even if freed and "repatriated" slaves had still no ties to Africa – families and communities that they could still remember, or who could identify them – these were liable to be scattered widely throughout western and central Africa. The slave trade to the Americas had of course been centered on the Atlantic coast of Africa, but with numerous centers from which slaves were bought. The slave trade also extended far into the interior.

Therefore, merely sending former slaves to Africa did not, in any real sense, constitute "sending them home," even for those relatively few whose former African homes might be identifiable. As was discussed above, this proved impossible even for those who were freed from slave ships, perhaps only days or weeks after having been seized from their homes.

For the white promoters of repatriation, it was a satisfying way to believe that they were righting a wrong without having to face up to the reality that African-Americans were fellow Americans. For the "repatriated" former slaves, it was not a return home, but was at least an opportunity to start new lives in a new country away from pervasive prejudice in the homeland to which their forebears had been brought in chains.

III. The Emergence of Liberia

Origins

The American Colonization Society was endorsed from the outset by distinguished names, such as President James Monroe – after whom Liberia's capital city of Monrovia was named – as well as General (and future president) Andrew Jackson, and then-Congressman and future Senator Daniel Webster. The promoters of the American Colonization Society did not succeed in their effort to have the federal government fully underwrite the effort, but did obtain an appropriation of $100,000, a very substantial sum at that time (Liebenow, 1987, p. 13).

In 1821, the repatriation project was ready to proceed. The first colonization ship, the *Elizabeth*, was accompanied by the USS *Cyane*, a further indication of US government interest in the project. An initial attempt to establish a settlement on Sherbro Island near Sierra Leone was unsuccessful, but a second effort in April of 1822 proved to be a success. The landing site for this settlement was chosen by another famous figure, Lieutenant, later Commodore Matthew Perry, who, two decades later, led the expedition that "opened" Japan to the outside world.

What was to be Liberia thus came into being. Unfortunately, relations with the indigenous people of the region got off on a poor footing even before the settlement near the future site of Monrovia was established. Leaders of the local Bassa and Dei tribes had obvious reason to be suspicious of this sudden appearance of Europeans – even if accompanied by people of African appearance. Their suspicions were in fact well-grounded since the settlers did not think of themselves as Africans, but as Americans (Taryor, 1985, p. 35).

Nevertheless, the local chieftains were eventually persuaded to sell the land on which the colony was to be established in return for $300 in muskets, tobacco, rum, and other goods (Liebenow, 1987, p. 16). However, there was a fundamental mutual misunderstanding – often to be repeated – over just what this "sale" implied. The Bassa and Dei, like many other tribal people , had no system of private land ownership; land was held communally.

It is not clear at this distance in time whether the indigenous leaders presumed that they were offering the colonists something like a "lease" to use land that would remain the ultimate property of their own communities, or whether – more corruptly – they were in the equivalent position of a mayor "selling" part of his city and pocketing the proceeds. Similar misunderstandings, or misdeeds, had occurred from the outset of English settlement in North America in dealing with the native American Indians, and such dubious transactions would continue to feature in the development of Liberia.

The first de-facto American overseas colony was thus established in Africa over three-quarters of a century before the Spanish-American War inaugurated what is conventionally regarded as the era of American overseas expansion. Another separate settlement was also established in 1832 by the Maryland State Colonization Society, which had broken away from the parent American Colonization Society. This settlement was located some distance south along the coast in what became Maryland County. This colony was not annexed to Liberia until 1862.

Growth

The new colonies, however, grew only gradually. By 1867, about 19,000 immigrants had been established in Liberia, including about a thousand in Maryland County (Liebenow, 1986, p. 19). Most of the immigrants can be divided into three roughly equal groups: those who were already free (including some former slaves who had purchased their freedom), others who were emancipated specifically in order to emigrate to Liberia, and captives who were rescued from salve ships and resettled in Liberia. Other immigrants were of varied origin. Over 300 arrived from Barbados in 1865, while no breakdown of the origins of the Maryland County immigrants is recorded. After the Civil War, between 1865 and 1904, some 4000 black Americans also emigrated to Liberia.

The "recaptives," settlers recaptured from slave ships, fit poorly into the Liberian colonial society. Unlike the American free blacks and emancipated slaves, they spoke no English, and their own origins varied widely. Known as "Congoes," they drifted to the bottom of the colonial social order (though still above the indigenous population).

Through the vagaries of language usage, however, "Congo" later became the term used by indigenous Liberians for all of the Americo-Liberian and other immigrants. The relationship between the Americo-Liberians, including "Congoes," with the indigenous societies of Liberia will be taken up later in this study.

Black Colonialism

The artificiality of repatriatiation as a concept has already been discussed above. As nascent Liberia began to take form, further implications began to take form that could have scarcely been imagined by either the white supporters of repatriation or the "repatriated" black Americans who settled in Liberia.

Few, if any, of their ancestors had come from the region that was now becoming Liberia. Even if by chance some had, all traces of the connection had been lost in the generations since the ancestors' enslavement. The immigrant settlers were black Americans, English-speaking Protestants. Apart from a generally dark skin tone, they had absolutely nothing in common with the

indigenous population with which they now come into contact —
not language, nor culture, nor religion, nor anything else that would
encourage them to form a common bond with their new neighbors.
The settlers had no more connection to the indigenous population of
Liberia than contemporary white American settlers in the West had
to the indigenous Indians.

Moreover, the settlers were products of their own time and
culture. What is now called multiculturalism was an unknown
concept to European or American society in the 19th century.
Western, Christian society was presumed to be inherently superior
to all others. More generally, a very strong distinction was drawn
between civilization – in the form of towns and cities, written laws,
then-modern technology, and so forth, and the presumed barbarism
or savagery of tribal societies.

To the Americo-Liberian settlers, the indigenous people
around them were savages – lacking all the customs and paraphernalia
that the settlers' own cultural background had taught them to associate
with civilization. In contrast, they themselves were civilized: literate,
sometimes fairly well educated, accustomed to taking for granted
such things as towns and law codes.

Thus, they regarded the indigenous people around them
in much the way that European colonialists of that era regarded
African and other tribal people (and even other non-tribal but non-
Western people): as "natives." Accordingly, the Americo-Liberian
settlers dealt with the indigenous Liberians much as colonialists

everywhere dealt with "native" – with a mixture of paternalism and raw exploitation.

These were the two patterns of behavior, both already well-established in the 1840s, for European colonial treatment of native populations. Simple exploitation was obvious enough, and both extremely widespread and systematic. Among the things that made the colonialists "civilized" was the possession of guns and military or quasi-military organization.

Colonialism had been established in the first place by military superiority, and this was as much the case in Liberia as elsewhere. The settlers had guns, as all colonialists did, and so had an overwhelming advantage over opponents armed only with traditional weapons, or even with the few guns they might be able to obtain. They could subjugate populations and force them into labor, or drive them out and seize their land, more or less at will. In Liberia the Americo-Liberians primarily did the former, for reasons to be discussed below.

Paternalism

Something should be said, however, of the "progressive" side of colonialism, paternalism, which was also widespread among European colonialists of the time. A variant on regarding natives as mere savages was to regard them as children, who would be taught civilized ways under the tutelage of the colonialists. Paternalist colonialism was at this time closely associated with the missionary movement.

If a "native" was converted to Christianity, he or she was implicitly acknowledged as a fellow child of God – even if not quite an equal one. Missionary efforts were closely associated with schooling, at least to teach converts to read the Bible (often translated by missionaries into the local language). This in turn was often extended to teaching the other rudiments of Western knowledge and civilized living.

The relationship between colonial paternalism and raw exploitation was a complex one. Paternalists often believed that, in principle, "natives" could be raised to the Western level. They often presumed, however, that this would take generations, and deferred it to an indefinite future. Nevertheless, they often opposed at least the harsher forms of colonial exploitation, and sometimes resisted with considerable courage. At the same time, on the other hand, paternalism and exploitation often went hand in hand – labor exploitation sometimes being justified as a means of teaching the natives civilized values such as the virtue of hard work.

The abolitionist movement in the United States, of which repatriation was one offspring, was closely bound up with the evangelical, missionary Protestantism of the time. Thus, it is no surprise that the ideology of paternalism took early root in Liberia.

Exploitation

At the same time, however, the element of raw exploitation was also present from the outset. The theory of repatriation, insofar as it had one, was that the America-Liberian settlers would become independent small farmers on the Jeffersonian model. This was a prevalent American ideal of the time, embodied in the various homestead laws, and which shaped much of the settlement of the American West.

Few America-Liberians, however, had any experience with homestead-style farming, or indeed any desire to become farmers. In any case, a large proportion were of urban origin and knew nothing at all of agriculture. Even those who had been emancipated from plantations tended for the most part to be former house slaves. These were the most likely to possess some education and skills, and were also more likely to be freed by their masters than were field hands. If they had any previous experience of agriculture at all, it was as slave labor – which embodied everything they wanted to get away from.

Attempts to establish the America-Liberians as farmers were thus almost uniformly unsuccessful. In addition to their general lack of prior farming experience, whatever they did know, or were taught, was liable to be unsuited to farming in the African environment.

The only group who had much success as farmers in Liberia were the "Congoes," the recaptives from slave ships. These had often been farmers before they were sold into slavery and they, at least knew something about farming African crops in African conditions, even if not the specific environment of Liberia.

What most of the Americo-Liberians did have experience with, and knew something about, was the operation of plantations. Thus a natural course of action for them – thrust into a new land, and finding there an indigenous population that was unable to resist them – was to re-establish the plantation system that they themselves had been freed from. Now, however, they could cast themselves in the role of their former masters.

That freed slaves would choose to establish a plantation system is of course paradoxical. Of all people, we might expect them to be most passionately opposed to slavery in all its forms and manifestations. All too often in history, however, oppressed groups have turned to oppressors as soon as the opportunity arose. The New England Puritans, who fled religious intolerance only to establish an intolerant rule of their own, are one familiar example from American history.

Moreover, no society appears out of a vacuum. The Americo-Liberians, in creating a society in their new country, fell back on the only example they knew, but from which they had been excluded from full membership – which was the society of the pre-Civil War South. This therefore became the model on which Americo-Liberian society was based:

Their standards were those of the antebellum American South. Far from rejecting the institutions, values, dress, and speech

21

of a society that had rejected them, the free persons of color painstakingly attempted to reproduce that culture on an alien shore. What they had rejected, apparently, was a situation that denied them full participation in American society (Liebenow, 1987, p. 23).

IV. Liberia and the United States

From its foundation, Liberia has been related to the place of a stepchild in American foreign policy and international relations. In spite of its special position as a quasi-colony, a center of American cultural influence, and potentially of American political influence on another continent, the history of US-Liberian relations has been largely one of sheer neglect.

This is often perplexing to Liberians. They share a language with Americans; their history is bound up with that of the United States; their capital is named for an American president – yet many Americans are only vaguely aware that Liberia exists, and know practically noting at all of either its history or present condition.

A primary reason for this neglect, at least for the first century of Liberia's independence, was undoubtedly racism. Liberia's population was almost entirely black, as was its ruling elites. (In fact, a gradation of color has often been socially significant, with the "bright-skinned" at the top of the status hierarchy. White Americans, however, rarely make such distinctions, or are even aware of them, regarding Liberians simply as "black.")

As was noted earlier in this discussion, "repatriation" of former slaves to Africa gained support in the first place due to the assumption that black Americans should not and probably could not be fully integrated into American life. Those same attitudes resulted in Liberia being regarded as less than a fully equal member of the family of nations.

This pattern began even more independent when the United States did not formally acknowledge Liberia as a colony or territory in spite of the involvement of President Monroe and numerous other prominent public figures in the American Colonization Society, not even after its independence in 1847. It was not until the presidency of Abraham Lincoln that Liberia was granted formal recognition by the United States – it being regarded as socially impossible to have a black envoy in Washington, DC.

Certainly, Liberia did not receive the privileged status then or later that would surely have been granted to a nation with a substantial population of white American settlers. Such a country would almost certainly enjoy a "special relationship" with the United States, somewhat as Britain and Israel do, in both cases partly because of ethnic ties to segments of the American population. Its security would be a US national priority, and its affairs would be heavily reported in the American mass media. None of these favored conditions apply to Liberia, whose historical ties to the United States are rarely mentioned.

Other non-racial factors, however, also perhaps contributed to American Neglect of Liberia. First and foremost of these was geography. Liberia was not in the Western Hemisphere, "America's backyard," but in distant West Africa. In the 19th century, US strategic foreign interests were regarded as limited primarily to the Western Hemisphere.

This principle was embodied in the famous Monroe Doctrine – promulgated during the administration of the same president for whom Monrovia is named – that the United States would not accept foreign (i.e., European) interference in the Americas. No such doctrine was ever considered for Africa or other continents.

In fact, till nearly the end of the 19th century, the United States was hardly in a position to enforce even the Monroe Doctrine. Except during the Civil War, it had only a small army. In spite of the role of the US Navy in suppressing the slave trade, and indeed directly in the establishment of the first Americo-Liberian settlement, the navy was even smaller, and could not have challenged any major European fleet.

This situation, in fact, was the immediate trigger of Liberian independence. In the 1840s, Liberian interests were encroached upon by the British colonial government in Sierra Leone, which denied Liberian land claims and intervened on behalf of European traders who refused to pay Liberian customs fees. The British refused to recognize the sovereignty of the American Colonization Society, and American protests were feeble or pro-forma. In response, the Americo-Liberians took matters into their own hands, issuing a Declaration of Independence in 1847 and proclaiming the Independent Republic of Liberia.

Even in the New World, the Monroe Doctrine itself survived for its first seven decades mainly because it was tacitly accepted by Great Britain, which had no desire to establish additional colonies in the New World and had the naval power to keep any other country from doing so. Although troubles with Britain had precipitated formal Liberian Independence, by the later 19th century, Britain was also the *de facto* protector of Liberia.

At the time of Liberia's establishment, the European presence in Africa was confined to the coasts, and was largely informal, exercised through various local leaders. In the 1870s and 1880s, however, the major European nations engaged in a competitive land-grab, in the course of which nearly the entire African continent was partitioned among the various colonial powers.

By 1900, the only independent African countries were Liberia and Ethiopia. Ethiopia was protected by its remoteness, and the failure of an Italian attempt to conquer and colonize it. Liberia was protected by Britain's willingness to accept the status quo in order to avoid seeing it colonized by a rival such as France. A British effort to annex Liberia might have brought a protest from the United States, but more importantly there was no need to do so.

Even when the United States became a major world power after 1900, Africa remained largely remote from American diplomatic concerns. Still dominated by the European colonial powers, it was regarded as a European sphere of influence. During World War II, as will be noted below, Monrovia became a staging base of some value for operations in the South Atlantic and North Africa but, it remained far from the main theaters of war and the American presence there remained limited.

Colonialism retained its hold on most of Africa until after World War II. Only in the years around 1960 did most former African colonies become independent nations. Even then, Africa remained something of a sideshow in the Cold War.

Africa was too far from the Soviet Union to face any direct threat, while most of its exports, such as coffee, lacked the strategic importance of such commodities as oil from the Middle East. When conflicts in Africa showed signs of Soviet influence, the United States was happy for the most part to allow the former Western colonial powers to take the lead in resisting that influence.

Otherwise, all that the United States looked for in Africa – as in most parts of the Third World – were governments that were reliably anti-Communist. So long as opposition to Communism and the Soviet Union was ensured, American official concern about economic development or human rights seldom rose above the level of lip service.

In this narrow view, the status quo in Liberia was regarded as quite satisfactory. Successive presidents of the True Whig party, all drawn from and representing the interests of the Americo-Liberian elites, could be counted on to oppose Communism at home, abroad, and to vote with the US against the Soviets in the United Nations. So long as they did so, the United States was happy to support them.

Dr. J. Mamadee Ghorpu-Dolo Woah-Tee, Sr.

The development of Liberian-American relations in modern times will be taken up further below.

V. The Development of Liberia

As noted previously, Liberia itself had many of the characteristics of a colonial power in Africa. The Americo-Liberians might have darker skin tones than European colonialists, but they shared quite similar attitudes toward "natives." The dubious terms of "sale" by which the Americo-Liberians acquired lands from indigenous leaders have already been mentioned in the context of the initial settlement.

The Americo-Liberians emulated European colonialists in other respects as well. At an early date, they instituted an institution of "wardship," or apprenticeship, whereby members of the indigenous population were taken on as household servants by Americo-Liberian families. The experience of these wards varied widely.

In some cases, they were adopted as full members of the families whose households they entered. (The same was quite generally true of the offspring of liaisons between Americo-Liberian men and indigenous women, who were regarded as family members, sharing for example in inheritances.) In other cases, however, wards were little more in effect than household slaves.

The Americo-Liberians also resembled European colonialists in their public policies toward the tribal communities around them. ("Tribe," a term disapproved of in most of Africa, is still in general use in Liberia.) In the best Livingston and Stanley style, the Americo-Liberians laid claim to lands and people they had "discovered." One young surveyor, Benjamin J.K. Anderson, after a journey to the inland Mandingo city of Musardu in 1868, described his adventures in fine, quite characteristic account of 19th century colonial exploration in the Dark Continent (Liebenow, 1987, p. 26).

Likewise, the Liberian government established colonial-style protectorate relationships with indigenous tribal groups and "alliances" that evolved into instruments of colonial subjugation. Following a particularly British pattern, the Americo- Liberians preferred to establish indirect rule over the tribes, through local chiefs who held their places only upon approval of the Liberian President in Monrovia.

Not until the 20th century were the indigenous tribal people granted even nominal status as Liberian citizens, and not until after 1944, with the reforms associated with President William V.S. Tubman (who served in office from 1944-1971) was any effort made to integrate them into Liberian society. These reform efforts, and their consequences, will be discussed below.

Meanwhile, one of the most serious crises in Liberian history erupted in 1927-29, when it was revealed that the Liberian government had colluded in obtaining indigenous workers to be sent to the Portuguese island of Fernando Po, where they were subjected to forced labor under very harsh conditions that amounted to slavery. The Fernando Po revelations erupted into an international scandal

– the more so because it involved a nation that was one of only two independent countries in Africa, and whose national motto proudly asserted that "The Love of Liberty Brought Us Here."

The situation drew the attention of the League of Nations and for a time, the real possibility existed that Liberia's Independence would be abrogated, and the nation reduced to a League Mandate. A settlement was eventually reached that preserved Liberia as an independent nation, though President Charles D.B. King was forced to resign. *The Crisis*, the magazine of the NAACP, noted with some irony that while Liberia had been censured for providing slave labor, Spain was not censured for using slave labor in its colony (Cimente, 1998, p. 40).

VI. Liberia in Transition

Liberian Politics

The beginning of the modern phase of Liberian history may be dated to 1944, with the accession of President William V.S. Tubman, who instituted a major program of reform. Before discussing Tubman's reforms and their consequences, something should be said of the Liberian political system as it existed until 1980.

The political institutions of the Liberian Republic were modeled, not unsurprisingly, on those of the United States, with a President, a Congress, and a Supreme Court. For the first few decades of independence, Liberia also had a multi-party system along typical American lines of the time. (It should be remembered that the two-party system only took full hold in the United States after the Civil War.)

These parties likewise took on names typical of American political parties of the time, such as Republican and Whig. (The first Republican Party in the United States was Jefferson's party, the lineal ancestor of today's Democratic Party.) In the 1860s, another party rose to prominence, the True Whig Party. This was initially a reformist party, associated particularly with the poorer,

Dr. J. Mamadee Ghorpu-Dolo Woah-Tee, Sr.

darker-skinned Americo-Liberians and "Congoes," who resisted the dominance of the "bright-skinned" ruling elites.

True Whig Dominance

By the 1870s, however, the Americo-Liberian elite as a whole, was increasingly conscious that it was greatly outnumbered by the indigenous people of its own country, and also, increasingly threatened by the rising tide of European imperialism around it. At about this same time, Americo-Liberian prosperity also underwent a sharp decline, partly because of the global depression of the time, and partly because Americo-Liberian traders, formerly very active along the African coast, were increasingly locked out by colonial preferences for their own nationals.

In these conditions, the Americo-Liberians closed ranks. They sacrificed political pluralism at home in order to present a united front against both the indigenous tribal people and the European colonialists who surrounded Liberia. After 1877, Liberian elections ceased to be seriously contested. In fact, the True Whig Party developed into the first instance of the one-party rule that has been so characteristic of modern, post-colonial Africa.

The Indigenous Liberians Under True Whig Rule

The indigenous population of Liberia was and is divided among 16 major ethnic and cultural groupings, or "tribes." Recent data on tribal populations are not available. The following tabular compilation dates as far back as 1974 (Liebenow, 1987, p. 35), and thus may greatly understate current population levels; however the relative proportions among different tribes are much less likely to have changed dramatically.

Kpelle	298,532	20 percent
Bassa	214.143	14
Gio	130,360	9
Kru	121,414	8
Grebo	119,985	8
Mano	110,770	7
Loma	88,351	6
Krahn	71,177	5
Gola	67,819	4 percent
Mandingo	58,414	4
Kissi	51,318	3
Vai	49,504	3
Gbandi	38,548	3
Mende	8,678	0.5
Belle	7,309	0.5
Dei	6,365	0.5 percent

In addition, the 1974 data list 3,141 "miscellaneous" tribal people, 14,706 "alien Africans," and 34,834 persons with no tribal affiliation. This last group, comprising 2.9 percent of the population at that time, may be taken as equivalent to the Americo-Liberians at that time still largely unchallenged as the Liberian elites.

Until the reforms of the Tubman era and the extensive road and railroad construction that accompanied them, much of the indigenous population of the interior had minimal contact with the Americo-Liberians – encountering few other than soldiers, tax collectors, and other officials. They thus had little interaction with the Liberian state, and still less interaction of any positive character. Writing in the late 1980s, J. Gus Liebenow observed that

Even today – despite the significant acceleration of social change under the Tubman, Tolbert, and Doe regimes – many (it not most) Liberians still identify much more strongly with their ethnic subcommunities than they do with the modern Liberian state (1987, p. 35).

Liberia resembled other African colonial states in all but the skin tone of the ruling elites. This applied likewise to its territorial boundaries. As elsewhere in colonial Africa, these were based in the first place on "sale" by local chieftains, claims based on "discovery," and simple imposition of Liberian authority. In a number of cases, this imposition did not occur until well into the 20th century. At various dates in the later 19th and early 20th centuries, some borders were modified – uniformly to Liberia's disadvantage – by pressure from neighboring European colonial territories.

In no case did these borders take any account of the indigenous population and its tribal divisions. Thus, as throughout Africa, the borders were and are artificial, cutting across ethnic lines.

Only a few of the ethnic groups, such as the Bassa, the Belle, and the Dei, are found almost entirely within Liberia. The majority of the sixteen [tribes] straddle the borders between Liberia and the neighboring states of Sierra Leone, Guinea, and the Ivory Coast. In some cases, such as the Mende, the major portion of the group resides across the border (Liebenow, 1987, pp. 34-35).

The Americo-Liberian elites employed various means to assert and maintain its control over the indigenous population. As in so many other respects, these had much in common with the methods used by European imperialists in the same era. The use of "sale" by chiefs, and of indirect rule through chiefs has already been mentioned.

These methods of maintaining control were reinforced in the Liberian case, however, by certain Americo-Liberian social customs that differed substantially from contemporary customs among most European imperialists. From an early date, Americo-Liberian men (and sometimes women) entered into liaisons with members of the indigenous tribes. Nothing, of course, was unusual in this; imperialists everywhere tended to take "native" wives or mistresses, without in any way revising their general low opinion of "natives."

However, as noted previously, the Americo-Liberians did not assign an inferior status to the offsprings of non-marital unions.

37

These children were, in general, treated as full family members and co-inheritors. Thus, a significant proportion of indigenous blood did enter the family trees of even the most elite Americo-Liberian families.

Such connections were often with the families of tribal chiefs or sub-chiefs, which formed an element of interconnection between those indigenous families and the Americo-Liberians. These were too few ever to produce any general intermingling of the people as a whole into a single national community, but it did strengthen the instrumentality of chiefly rule as a means of securing Americo-Liberian dominance.

Other means of control ranged from sheer military force to the imposition of travel restrictions on tribal members in effect confining them to "Bantustans" within Liberia. Another instrument of control, widespread elsewhere in Africa, was the imposition of a hut tax, and compulsory labor service.

Labor service included enforced labor on roads and other public works, often under very harsh conditions. It also included what came to be called the "portage" system, whereby indigenous people were required to carry visiting Americo-Liberian officials about the countryside in sedan chairs. This last imposition, though in itself less severe than other forms of labor service, was particularly detested because of its humiliating connotations.

Liberian Economic Development

Some of the white supporters of the American Colonization Society had dreamed of establishing a Jeffersonian society of small farmers in Liberia. As was noted earlier, this quickly fell by the wayside. Few America-Liberians had neither the training or inclination to become small farmers. Among the settlers, only the "Congoes," still themselves Africans, had much success as farmers.

In the early decades, the Americo-Liberians had considerably more success as traders.

They gradually displaced the Mandingoes and even the European merchants and monopolized the trade between the coast and the interior. Among tribal persons and Westerners alike, the Americo-Liberian trader enjoyed a reputation as a shrewd bargainer who exchanged the cloth, rum, and tobacco from America and Europe for the camwood, can sugar, palm kernels, rice, and the occasional ivory tusk that tribal traders brought to the coast. Often the enterprising Americo-Liberian trader – at risk to his own life – ventured up the rivers in search of trade items (Liebneow, 1987, p. 22).

In the process, a significant Liberian merchant marine grew up. In modern times Liberia has been known almost entirely as a flag of convenience for foreign-owned ships, most of which have never entered a Liberian port. Between 1848 and 1871, however, 139 Liberian-owned merchant ships are recorded (Leibenow, 1987,

p. 75). The captains and many crew members of these ships, as well as their owners, appear to have been Americo-Liberians.

However, events from the 1870s on acted to stifle this Liberian commercial enterprise. As was noted earlier in this discussion, the general global depression of the times, and imperial preferences by various colonial powers for their own nationals were contributing factors. Another was the spread of steamships.

The Liberian ships were sailing vessels, predominantly schooners. Americo-Liberian traders had the capital to purchase such ships, and their captains and crews had the skills to work them. Steamships, however – though more profitable in the long run – were more expensive initially, and required industrial and technical resources not readily available in Liberia. The Liberians could not compete against steam, and their trade further dwindled.

The economic effect was to undermine Liberian prosperity in the late 19th century. The social effect was to undermine it far into the 20th century, by turning the Americo-Liberian elites away from economic activity to a nearly exclusive focus on law and government. They thus became parasitical on the very state that they controlled. The basic means by which members of the elite made money was by using their control of the political levers to steer preference their way.

Most business activity was in the hands of Europeans, other Africans, and Lebanese. Thus, in the 1960s, more than 80 percent of firms in Montserrado County (in which Monrovia is situated) were foreign-owned. The Liberian-owned companies tended either to be marginal small businesses, or fronts in which an Americo-Liberian was listed as owner of a firm actually run by foreigners.

Members of the Americo-Liberian elites were likewise sprinkled among the board members of foreign companies doing business in Liberia, where they served as political fixers (Liebenow, 1987, pp. 77-78). While it is common enough around the world for business owners to become involved in politics in order to further their business interests, the practice in Liberia was rather for the Americo-Liberians to become involved in business only in order to profit from their political connections.

VII. The Tubman Era

President Tubman was a member in good standing of the uppermost stratum of Americo-Liberian society. Typically of his class, he had held a succession of public offices in the course of the political ascent that brought him to the presidency. In his earlier career, however, he had been a lawyer. In his practice, he had often defended poor clients, including members of the indigenous tribal communities, against powerful members of the elites.

This background perhaps made Tubman more aware of the rising tide of nationalism that was starting to row around Africa from the 1920s on. Like other members of the Americo-Liberian elite, Tubman was acutely aware of the essentially colonial nature of the Liberian society and, the potential risks to Americo-Liberians control and privilege that might be posed by the political awakening of Liberia's indigenous majority.

Tubman's Reform Policies

Unlike most of his peers, however, President Tubman was prepared to take positive steps to manage this situation before it got out of hand. His "Open Door" policy had two essential components.

The first component was opening up Liberia to much wider participation by foreign economic interests. Tubman realized that the Americo-Liberians, their entrepreneurial instincts long since dulled, lacked both the capital and the will to develop Liberia's economic potential effectively. By inviting in foreign capital, Tubman sought to jump-start the development of resources such as Liberia's extensive deposits of iron ore.

The other component of the Open Door policy – subsequently furthered by a Unification Program – was to offer some degree of participation to the indigenous population. The franchise had nominally been extended to the tribal people in the early 20th century, when this measure had been viewed as necessary to buttress Liberia's territorial integrity against the threat of encroachment by the surrounding colonial powers.

However, the extension of the franchise had been limited by a property requirement that few tribal members could meet. Moreover, the practice had developed of allowing tribal leaders to cast their entire communities' votes en bloc. Tubman abolished this practice, introducing individual balloting. He also greatly reduced the property requirement, opening the franchise to all tribal members who paid the hut tax. In addition, under the Unification Program he abolished the legal distinctions that had previously set apart the indigenous people from the Americo-Liberians, denying full political status to the vast majority of the population.

The political map of Liberia was also redrawn. From the 19th century on, the coastal region of Liberia had been divided into four counties. These were the functional equivalent of American states, electing Senators and Representatives. The interior, however, had been divided into three provinces, to which only minimal representation was assigned.

Tubman increased interior representation. Then, in 1964, he reorganized the entire structure, carving up the interior provinces into four additional counties, that elected Senators and Representatives as the coastal counties did (Liebenow, 1987, pp. 64-65). Representation was however quite unequal, the interior being under-represented, while Monserrado County, with Monrovia, was sharply over-represented. Nevertheless, the new political map at least gave some recognition to the tribal interior as a full part of Liberia.

Both components of the Open Door policy were supported by an extensive program of infrastructure improvements, particularly construction of new roads, bridges, and railroads, and by some efforts, to extend public services into the interior of the country. President Tubman regarded these investments as necessary to carry out both primary elements of the Open Door policy. On the one hand, the new roads and rail lines would encourage foreign investment in Liberia. On the other hand, they would further integrate the country itself.

The Limits of Reform

The actual effects of Tubman's reform on the indigenous population were mixed. The significance of extending the franchise was obviously limited by the one-party character of Liberia, with all levels of political life dominated by the True Whigs. The franchise was not purely nominal in spite of the absence of contested elections. The True Whig Party, like many ruling parties in one-party states, did have a participatory element. Through party activity such as attendance at caucuses, members could in fact have some influence on political decision-making.

However, while the effect was to open a path to some political participation by individuals, the one-party nature of the system placed sharp limits on the scope of public discussion and debate. Those who joined the True Whig Party and took part in its activities might open a path for their own political advancement, but they did so by conforming. They rarely offered new voices that would challenge the existing order.

On the economic side, the effects of economic development were uneven, and – as often in Third World countries – the majority of the population felt the burdens more than the benefits of economic growth. For example, the opening up of the interior by road construction hastened a new wave of land-acquisition by the

Americo-Liberian elites. New pressures were thus imposed on tribal populations.

The development of agriculture was also disrupted by the policy of subsidizing food prices in Monrovia. The subsidies served to placate the growing, under-employed restless urban population, who might pose the most immediate threat to the established order. In fact, as will be seen below, an increase in the price of subsidized rice in 1979 was a major precipitating event to the coup of 1980.

However, the urban food-price subsidy also reduced the price available to farmers growing food crops for local consumption. At the same time, subsidies were paid to the largely-absentee Americo-Liberian owners of plantations growing cash crops for export. The results were rural poverty, pressure on rural cultivators to move to the cities in search of (often nonexistent) jobs, and an increasing dependence on imported food.

However, these limitations and shortcomings should not lead us to underestimate the real transformation that occurred in Liberia during the Tubman and Tolbert eras, between 1944 and 1980. Liberia became a more fully integrated nation than it had been, and in closer touch with the world. It was estimated by one group of economists that, by 1980, the economy's growth "provided relatively high-income wage employment for over one-third of the adult male population in the country – a higher proportion than in most low-income LDCs [less developed countries]" (Liebenow, 1987, p. 163).

Education had also expanded greatly. Schools in the interior, previously almost exclusively the province of missionary efforts, had been greatly expanded. While the overall literacy rate was only 20-25 percent, between 1960 and 1980 the rate of primary school enrollment increased from 31 percent to 66 percent, while secondary school enrollment went from 2 percent to 20 percent. In 1960, according to J. Gus Liebenow (1987, p. 162), the city of Monrovia had only one bookstore. On a return visit in 1980, he counted over twenty, with a wide range of materials available.

With development, however, came a revolution of rising expectations. This was ultimately what doomed Tubman's successor in the presidency, William R. Tolbert, and the entire established Americo-Liberian dominated social order. In 1944, Tubman had sensed the tide of change that was gradually rising across Africa. At that time, however, few Liberians outside of the elites – whether the poorer Americo-Liberians or the vast indigenous majority – could have given a name to the sources of their discontent.

By the 1970s, however, for all the real progress that had been made, Liberians had a far clearer picture of what had not been accomplished. They were aware of their country's severely uneven development, and of the heavy hand of the still-dominant Americo-Liberian elites and their political instrument, the True Whig Party. As so often in history, the very process of reform fanned the flames that would develop into revolution.

Liberian-American Relations in the Tubman Era

The relationship between Liberia and the United States has, as outlined, been one of stepchild and step-parent from the outset. Even formal recognition was not granted until the presidency of Abraham Lincoln, lest Washington be compelled to endure a black envoy. Nevertheless, the United States had generally spoken up on Liberia's behalf when international controversies arose.

The low point of Liberian-US relations came in the wake of the Firestone scandal revelations of 1927-29. The League of Nations had come close to abrogating Liberian independence, while the United States stood by in silence. A cause was surely the nature of the revelations; it being held particularly shocking that a nation founded by former slaves should countenance *de facto* slavery. Another factor, however, may have been the implication of an American firm in the affair. This made it more political for the United States to adopt a tone of moral outrage.

Once the scandal ended, Liberian-US relations were mended. The relationships grew notably warmer with the accession of William V.S. Tubman to the presidency in 1944. In addition to the domestic reform initiatives outlined above, Tubman signaled solidarity with the western Allies by declaring war on the Axis powers. Liberia's contribution to the war effort was to provide the use of Monrovia as a US base where five thousand troops were stationed.

After the war, Liberia continued in the Western alignment. From the perspective of US diplomacy, Liberia was a useful pro-Western voice in Africa as the continent moved toward independence, and radical voices contended for influence with more moderate ones. Moreover, Liberia was the one country in Africa that had historical ties to the United States, for all that the latter rarely acknowledge those ties.

There were also more affirmative reasons for the United States to take renewed interest in Liberia. FDR and Truman, as well as later presidents such as JFK, all domestic reformers themselves, felt a natural affinity for the reform policies undertaken by President Tubman. His "Open Door" and "Unification" programs, though entirely of Tubman's own devising, had in both rhetoric and substance much the flavor of initiatives that might have been proposed by the US State Department.

The positive US response to these Tubman-era initiatives was undoubtedly sincere. It was, however, also naïve as well as somewhat self-interested. "Reforms," when accompanied by a strong stand against socialism, Communism, and the Soviet Union, were music to official American ears.

Moreover, American official or quasi-official visitors to Liberia rarely had much contact with Liberians beyond the Americo-Liberian elites, or with much of Liberia beyond Monrovia. In President Tubman and his circle, they found a group of well-educated, sophisticated individuals who spoke their language figuratively as well as literally, and who – at least rhetorically – shared American values. In the country, they saw visible signs of progress, in the form of new roads and bridges, and growing export production.

In the optimistic mid-century decades, the challenges to development in the Third World were moreover greatly underestimated, not only in the West but also by many leaders, including reform-minded ones in the Third World itself. Superficial indicators of progress tended in those years to be taken at face value. This proved to be the case not only in Liberia but also in Vietnam, Iran, and a host of other countries around the world.

The signs of imbalance and discontent were far less obvious to visitors who had little real knowledge of Liberia. The only members of the indigenous tribal majority of Liberians who such visitors were likely to meet were the small group of chiefs and others who had affiliated themselves with the True Whig party. The few Americans who had in-depth knowledge of Liberia were unlikely to have the official ear, or else had business interests in Liberia that aligned them with the Americo-Liberian elites.

VIII. Liberia in Crisis

The Tolbert Years

Villiam Tubman died in July of 1971, while undergoing surgery at a London hospital. He had been president for over a quarter of a century. His policy initiatives had transformed Liberia. The tribal interior, previously nearly inaccessible, had been opened up to coastal Liberia and, Liberia as a whole, had been opened up to the world. The indigenous people had been made full citizens, at least on paper, and politics was no longer the sole preserve of the Americo-Liberian elites.

At the same time, world events had transformed Africa. When Tubman came to office, Liberia was one of only two independent countries in Africa, the other being Ethiopia. The rest of the continent was under European colonial rule. (South Africa was semi-independent, but under white minority rule.) By 1971, colonial rule had ended safe in a few small enclaves and the continent as a whole, was in a ferment of change. It was clear that Liberia's future, like Africa's, would not resemble its past.

Tubman was succeeded in 1971 by Vice President William R. Tolbert. At the time, he was widely regarded as only an interim figure. While he had served as Tubman's vice president for five of the latter's six terms, he had been seen as a colorless functionary. It was anticipated that he would be replaced in the next election, probably by a member of Tubman's family or by one of his close associates (Liebenow, 1987, pp. 122-23).

Tolbert, however, proved to be a surprise. Previously known for being seen only in the formal attire of the Americo-Liberian elites, he was sworn into office wearing a short-sleeved shirt typical of African populist leaders of the time. He repeated his inaugural address in Liberian English, and replaced the presidential limousine with a Volkswagen.

Even more than Tubman, Tolbert established a reputation for making his personal presence felt around the country, with frequent visits to all regions. He showed visible rapport in meeting tribal leaders and others. He carried forward the Unification program – which had stalled in the later Tubman years – for example by the final abolition of the province system and the reorganization of interior Liberia into counties.

Tolbert also proposed and carried through an important restructuring in the Liberian political structure, limiting the presidency to two terms, the first of eight and the second of four years. Previously, presidents had served an initial eight-year term, and been eligible for an unlimited number of following four-year terms, as in Tubman's long tenure.

This would have produced more frequent rotation in office and more flexible evolution of the Liberian political system. In the event, however, the "First Republic" was to be cut short – along with Tolbert's life – by the coup in 1980.

In fact, President Tubman had already transformed the Liberian political structure in a way that Tolbert continued. While Liberia had been a one-party state since the 1880s, controlled by the True Whig Party, it had not previously been dominated by the presidency. The primary branch of government had previously been the Congress. Several earlier presidents – including Tubman's immediate predecessor, Edwin J. Barklay – had been compelled to resign under threat of impeachment.

Through Tubman's long tenure in office, and continuing under Tolbert, the presidency became the dominant institution in Liberian politics. The Congress declined in significance, its debates lively but having little impact. The judiciary, nominally independent, had never effectively asserted itself.

Along with presidential dominance came a cult of presidential personality. This too developed steadily under Tubman, and continued under Tolbert. A growing number of roads and bridges were named for him, his statue appeared in most public places, and shops were required to have his picture on the wall.

Adulation of the president grew into a substantial financial burden on the country, such as "birthday presents" for which large deductions were made from public servants' salaries. Tolbert gradually gave into this cult.

Despite, however, his great start in continuing the humanization of the presidency which had been initiated by Tubman, Tolbert seemed incapable of sustaining the momentum. His initial populist posturing gradually gave way to all the trappings of royalty (Liebenow, 1987, pp. 120-121).

As a result, Tolbert was perhaps not clearly aware that social tensions in Liberia were continuing to grow. While the cultural barriers between the Americo-Liberians and the indigenous population were to some degree breaking down, the assimilation process was heavily tilted toward Americo-Liberian norms. Moreover, the gradual fusing of two communities only sharpened the element of socio-economic strain.

As early as 1962, a study team from Northwestern University characterized Liberia as undergoing "growth without development" (Liebenow, 1987, p. 165). Infrastructure had been built, but its operation was overwhelmingly in the hands of foreigners. The Liberian educational system, culminating with the University of Liberia, trained its students primarily as lawyers, with few of the technical skills needed to manage a developing country.

If the foreign operators were to leave, the Northwestern University study suggested, the Liberian infrastructure would simply collapse. Most alarmingly, the study concluded that "under present social and political arrangements, offering economic advice to Liberian leaders was rather futile" (Liebenow, 1987, pp. 165-66).

The End of True Whig Rule

The decline of agriculture was particularly severe, and ultimately became explosive. Between 1978 and 1981, importation of food grains – in primarily agricultural country – rose from 1300 metric tons to 226,300 metric tons (Liebenow, 1987, p. 169). As was noted previously, one factor in the weakness of the agricultural sector was the government's policy of holding down food prices in Monrovia. This alleviated tensions in the capital at the cost of undermining farmers, who could not receive an adequate price for their crop and thus had no incentive to bring it to market.

By 1979, this policy had led the Tolbert government into a vise, hemmed in by all sides. It could no longer afford the subsidy, and in April of 1979 announced that the price of a 50-pound sack of rice would double. Demonstrations known as the rice riots broke out on April 14, 1979. While National Guard (army) troops refused to fire on the crowd, the Monrovia city police panicked and did so, and dozens were killed (Liebenow, 1987, p. 1761).

The end of the True Whig Party, and President Tolbert personally, came almost exactly a year later on April 12, 1980. A group of enlisted soldiers led by Master Sergeant Samuel Kanyon Doe entered the presidential residence and killed Tolbert (Liebenow, 1987, pp. 184ff). According to one account they entered intending to demand back pay, found Tolbert asleep at his desk, and bayoneted him on the spot (Drury and Roston, 2001, p. 231-32).

Samuel Doe and the PRC

The True Whig rule collapsed at once and completely amid general rejoicing on the streets of Monrovia. To many Liberians, it seemed that their country had been reborn (Andrews, 1994, p. xvi). Doe proclaimed himself provisional head of state as leader of the People's Redemption Council (PRC). Ten days later the new government took its most dramatic early action by executing thirteen prominent figures associated with the Tolbert regime on a beach near Monrovia.

The executions, televised and carried out amid a carnival atmosphere, testified if nothing else to the new leadership's fundamental lack of sophistication (Liebenow, 1987, pp. 188-90). This did not bode well for their management of the Liberian government and economy. In the more immediate term, the spectacle led to an international outcry, and cast Liberia's foreign relations into doubt.

The PRC also flirted initially with a radical international orientation, notably with Libya. This flirtation, however, ended in 1982, marked by another execution. The victim this time was Major General Thomas Weh Syen, who had been Doe's second in command, and the most radical senior member of the PRC (Liebenow, 1987, p. 200).

The United States, whose perspective was inclined almost entirely in Cold War terms, was eager to welcome the prodigal stepson back to the anticommunist fold. In the course of the 1980s,

Liberia would be showered with some $500 million in US foreign aid (Drury and Roston, 2001, p. 232). In turn for this, the US was allowed to set up intelligence "listening posts" in Liberia, while Doe challenged other African leaders to fistfights for criticizing Ronald Reagan (Bright, 2002). Much of the aid money would end up in the hands of PRC officials (Andrews, 1993, p. xvii), as earlier aid had ended up in the hands of True Whig Party officials. The condition of the economy further deteriorated under PRC mismanagement (Sawyer, 1987, p. 7).

Nevertheless, Doe and the PRC commanded considerable public support in Liberia for several years, into the middle 1980s. As the economy declined, however, and a promised return to civilian rule was repeatedly delayed, support for the PRC gradually waned. Finally, in 1985, under considerable domestic and international pressure, elections were held.

The 1985 Elections

Samuel Doe was unsurprisingly a candidate for the presidency, running now under the banner of the National Democratic Party of Liberia (NDPL). His primary challenger emerged as Jackson Doe (no relation) and the Liberian Action Party, or LAP (Liebenow, 1987, pp. 272-79). In spite of various efforts by the government to disrupt opposition political activities, the election in 1985 was in itself perhaps the fairest and freest in Liberian history. Voting was heavy, and "exit polling" by the LAP indicated that it was running well in most of the country.

While the election itself had been fairly conducted, irregularities soon emerged in the vote count. Some Liberians reported having seen burned ballots scattered along highways. In the end, the NDPL and Samuel Doe were declared the winners, by 50.7 percent of the vote.

Few were taken in by this account in Liberia or elsewhere, though the US State Department declared its confidence in the result. Among other observers, it is generally accepted that Samuel Doe rigged the count, accepting a narrow margin of victory because claiming any wider one would have been even more unbelievable (Liebenow, 1987, p. 297).

Liberia's economic and political situation continued to deteriorate. In spite of the US endorsement of Samuel Doe's election, its active support for his regime was drawing to an end. The reason had nothing to do with the situation in Liberia, and everything to do with geopolitics.

The Cold War was drawing to an end and with it, the end of US strategic interest in Liberia as a base or as a listening post on Libya and South Africa. "'As soon as the Cold War was over,' a prominent Liberian said bitterly, 'the US didn't give a damn.'" (Drury and Roston, 2001, p. 232). The American Embassy, built up into a massive fortress in the 1980s, was soon reduced to a backwater with minimal staffing, as it remains to the present day.

World perception of the Doe government was forever established by the summary executions carried out in its first days in office, and by the theft of the 1985 election. However, these were only the most dramatic of the regime's civil and human rights violations.

Large numbers of Liberians were swept up and detained by the new government's security forces. These included not only individuals associated with the True Whig party, but also student leaders, journalists, and civilian political figures who had previously been critical of True Whig rule (*Promise Betrayed*, 1986, pp. 85-89). For those detained, prison conditions were execrable, with flogging of prisoners a regular practice (*Promised Betrayed*, p. 82).

The beginning of the Doe era had been marked by a brief "renaissance" in the early months following the coup that brought him to power (*Promise Betrayed*, p. 143). However, intimidation and repression of the press soon reached a more intensive level than had ever been seen in the True Whig era. Independent newspapers were regularly closed down, while journalists were taken into custody without charges, to be held for periods up to months (*Promise Betrayed*, pp. 144-48).

Nor was the press the only institutional victim. Repression of academic freedoms, traditionally respected in Liberia, culminated with an armed attack on the University of Liberia campus in 1985 (*Promise Betrayed*, p. 155). Distinguished academicians were forced into exile. Many ended up on the faculties of American universities where they could help make Americans more aware of the two nations' ties and of conditions in Liberia. However, this gain was more than offset by the loss of their services to the Liberian people.

Civil War, Chaos, and Charles Taylor

In 1989, Liberia was "invaded" by a band of some 100 fighters who crossed the border from the Ivory Coast, commanded by Charles Taylor. Taylor, of mixed indigenous and Americo-Liberian ancestry, had studied in the United States, and returned to Liberia in 1980 after the overthrow of the Tolbert regime. He joined the PRC government, but later fled again to the United States amid accusations of embezzlement. At one point he was arrested in the US and held for extradition in a Massachusetts jail, only to escape down a rope made of bedsheets.

Now he launched a civil war against the Doe regime. For the next seven years, Liberia descended into a chamber of horrors. The Doe government, recruited heavily from the Krahn tribe, had introduced a new element of tribal rivalry into Liberia (Bright, 2002). The civil war greatly exacerbated the situation, and tens of thousands died in the course of the fighting.

A pan-African peacekeeping force, made up predominantly of Nigerian troops, was sent to Liberia, but was unable to exert its authority beyond the capital. In the countryside, the fighting went on. Eventually Samuel Doe fell, accepting refuge in the stronghold of a local warlord who then executed him. Multi-factional fighting raged on, until

"In 1997, all sides in the Liberian conflict agreed to presidential elections. Taylor compiled, but his subtext was evident – if he lost, he would return to the bush to make war anew. Thus a battle-weary populace rallied around one of the most unusual election slogans in political history: 'You killed my ma, you killed my pa, I'll vote for you.'" (Drury and Roston, 2001, p. 233).

Predictably, Taylor won, and remained in power up to August 11, 2003. In 2001, the United Nations imposed sanctions on Liberia for human rights violations and his close ties to the brutal rebel movement in neighboring Sierra Leone.

One of the most peculiar recent developments in Liberia has been the involvement of Rev. Pat Robertson, former head of the Christian Coalition, the American conservative political-action group. Robertson, in working alliance with the Taylor regime, has obtained concessions for gold mining in Liberia. The Bush Administration, for which Robertson still represents an important constituency, has found it expedient to turn a blind eye to this activity.

"A current State Department official in the Bush Administration admits that he personally finds Robertson's relationship with Taylor 'despicable,' but allows that 'well, we are a capitalist society in a capitalist system'" (Drury and Roston, 2001, p. 234).

The cycle of American public and official indifference to its African stepchild thus continues at the present day. To be sure, the assertion made above might well be made about the activities of American business interests in many Third World countries. However, it is remarkable in being said with respect to the activities of a prominent public figure, with whom the administration has political ties. It is even more remarkable in being said of activities in a country founded by Americans, which the United States might be expected to feel special ties.

By the summer of 2003, the long-running Liberian civil war began turning more strongly against the Charles Taylor government. As the rebels advanced and Taylor's troops were forced to retreat, the humanitarian crisis that had already wracked Liberia for years became even more desperate. The conduct of both armies was characterized by indiscipline and brutality, and as the fighting became more fluid, more towns and villages were subjected directly to the horrors of warfare. Refugees in the tens of thousands began pouring into Monrovia.

At this point, the long-running human disaster in Liberia threatened to become a human catastrophe. If the fighting spilled directly into Monrovia, the civilian death toll might quickly swell into the hundreds of thousands. Starvation was already spreading, as the city – crowded now with a quarter million refugees – was cut off from food supplies (Wise, 2003). To add to the horror, rebel artillery began shelling the city. In this environment of imminent crisis, pressure grew for the international community to intervene.

In particular, there was a strong desire, inside and outside of Liberia, for the United States to lead an international effort to restore a minimal level of peace and security within Liberia, and to make possible a humanitarian intervention. There were several reasons why the United States was called upon to show leadership. The quasi-colonial historical relationships between the United States and Liberia was not the sole or even the principal reason for this call for action.

Instead, the primary reasons why the United States was asked to lead an intervention were first, its unmatched military and logistics capabilities, and second, the broad perception in Liberia and across much of Africa that the United States was most able to serve as an honest, disinterested broker. The first of these points, military and material capability, scarcely needs to be expanded upon. The forces that were fighting the Liberian civil war were both essentially armed rabbles that scarcely deserved to be called armies. Even a small force of well-equipped and well-disciplined troops would be able to suppress them.

The more important factor, however, was the respect and esteem held for the United States, among Liberians and other Africans. Through much of Africa, the United States is seen as able to serve as an honest broker, free of neo-colonial or other partisan motives. This contrasts, for example, to France, which has highly capable forces deployed in Africa, but is by no means viewed as a consistently honest and evenhanded party in African affairs.

65

Liberians in particular, as we have seen, are acutely aware of their ties to the United States, even if few Americans share this awareness. It is significant that as the fighting began to spill into Monrovia, Liberian refugees gathered around the American Embassy in Monrovia, as the one place where they might feel safe (Jelinek, 2003). At one point, however, even the embassy grounds came under shelling from rebel troops.

In this request for American-led intervention, there was no expectation that the United States would need to contribute the bulk of a peacekeeping force. African countries such as Nigeria stood ready to contribute a substantial force of well-trained professional troops. However, the performance of the Nigerians during the previous intervention in Liberia had been marred by numerous instances of misconduct. Thus, the presence of even a small number of American troops was seen a crucial in establishing the credibility of the entire projected force.

Unfortunately, the American administration proved extremely reluctant to make even a minimal commitment to restoring peace and security to Liberia (Jelinek, 2003). Several reasons might be offered for this reluctance.

It is certainly true that, in the summer of 2003, the United States military was severely stretched. The successful initial invasion of Iraq had given way to an unexpectedly difficult occupation. Contrary to the initial expectation that most of the American force could be quickly removed, the US troops in Iraq found themselves facing an ongoing insurgency, against which they were in fact short-handed. Thus, the United States did not have very many troops to spare.

However, while the American military as a whole might be stretched thin, the number of troops required for a Liberia intervention was quite small – a few hundred at most. In fact, sufficient troops were already available on the potential theater of operations; a US Navy amphibious ship with some 2000 Marines was stationed in the West African waters. The question for the American political leadership was thus not one of means but of will.

The precise reasons for the reluctance to intervene in Liberia will not be known until the archives of the Bush Administration are available to historians. However, these reasons may be reasonably inferred from the administration's overall conduct of and pronouncements regarding international affairs.

The second, Bush administration came to office with a deep-rooted hostility to multilateral humanitarian interventions abroad. In part, the administration and its supporters associated such policies with the preceding Clinton administration, which Bush's strongest political supporters had largely detested. More generally, the circles around Bush adhere to a narrow conception of American interests, limited by region and objectives. Specific American economic interests, such as access to Middle Eastern oil supplies, are judged worthy of military support. So are the strategic objectives of containing – and if possible overthrowing – a handful of governments identified as anti-American rogue states.

Liberia and the Taylor regime did not fall within this restrictive range of threats to American interests, as perceived by the Bush administration. As noted above, it happens that Rev. Pat Robertson, a political ally of Bush, had a personal economic stake in the Taylor regime. However, there are no grounds for supposing that this by itself was a factor in the administration's resistance to a Liberia intervention. It is much more probable that Liberia was disfavored as a "mere" humanitarian intervention.

Absent from this interpretation of American interests, however, is a recognition of the threat posed by "failed states," or the very real risk of anarchy and chaos spreading to envelop the entire regions, creating a breeding ground for terrorism. This reflects an outlook rooted in the conventional attitudes of the past. The experience of the last decade should have made clear that the real threat to the United States is posed not by states, but by shadowy groups that grow and thrive in conditions of disorder. If the civil war were left unchecked, Liberia might well become the Afghanistan of the next decade, a place from which terrorist groups could operate freely due to the absence of law and security.

In fact, the resistance of the Bush administration toward an intervention in Liberia may usefully be compared to its failure to adequately plan for the aftermath of the invasion of Iraq. The specific circumstances naturally differ, but they have in common a narrow interpretation of world politics as a sort of chessboard, on which the only relevant players are specific states posing specific threats to American interests. The presumption in Liberia was that neither Charles Taylor nor the anarchy that threatened to envelop the country were relevant threats. The presumption in Iraq was that with the overthrow of the Saddam Hussein regime, all the problems the United States had in Iraq would simply go away. In neither case was there a recognition of the complex interrelationships that operate in the contemporary world, or of the threat that disorder poses not only to local populations but to global security.

Fortunately, the Bush administration was finally pressured into permitting a very minimal level of commitment to Liberia. This pressure came particularly from Britain. Because Britain was one of the very few major allies the Americans had in Iraq, the British government was able to exert strong and effective pressure on American policymakers to provide some commitment to Liberia as well.

This commitment consisted of no more than about 100 Marines, who briefly landed by helicopter in Monrovia to conduct reconnaissance in preparation for the arrival of an African peacekeeping force. As minimal as it was, even this appearance by American troops provided the key to a diplomatic effort to remove Taylor from power.

Taylor was under indictment for his human rights abuses. However, there was no realistic prospect of apprehending him in the short term. Humanitarian workers and diplomats felt that the highest priority was to persuade him to step down and go into exile, rather than keep up a struggle for power that could only lead to further continued bloodshed. During June and July of 2003, several hundred civilians were slain in Monrovia (Jelinek, 2003). Up to thousands more elsewhere in the country were still falling victim to the civil war.

Negotiations for Taylor's exile were protracted. For several weeks, matters were at an impasse (Liberia's Fine Balance," 2003). Taylor refused to step down until peacekeeping troops arrived, but the African peacekeeping force was not willing to enter Monrovia while fighting rage din the capital. Even at this point, Taylor was no doubt hoping that he would somehow manage to cling to power.

However, after much wrangling – and faced with the final collapse of his power base – Charles Taylor finally abandoned Liberia and fled into exile in Nigeria on August 11, 2003 (Wise, 2003). His hand-picked vice president, Moses Blah, assumed the presidency until a new interim government could be established. Many suspected that Taylor still hoped to control the reins of power, even from exile, acting through Blah.

However, as of October 4, 2003, businessman Gyude Bryant returned from exile in Ghana to head the interim government, ending the brief administration of Moses Blah ("Expectations High," 2003). Bryant was chosen as a broker who would be able to negotiate among the various factions in Liberia. Liberia's long slide toward anarchy had been checked, and the long, difficult task of reconstruction had at least a chance to begin.

By any standard, the Charles Taylor regime was the worst that the unhappy land of Liberia has been forced to endure, not only in the past three decades but through the nearly two centuries of its history. While Samuel Doe ruled the country with a harsh, brutal hand, and undid much of the groundwork for development that had been laid, however imperfectly, during the presidencies of Tubman and Tolbert, he showed at least minimal competence at the basic tasks of government. His army and police were brutal, and his rule arbitrary, but ordinary Liberians still had some chance of living their lives in relative peace, and even some slight hope of building for a better future.

Historical experience, underlined in recent decades, has demonstrated that the one thing worse than tyrannical government is no government at all, a state of anarchy in which everyday life becomes impossible. This is the state of affairs that Taylor visited upon Liberia. He combined a brutality and abuse of power at least as great as Doe's with an utter inability to provide even the most minimal level of security.

The murder of some half a million Liberians under his regime, as horrific as it is, is in a sense only the most visible indicator of Taylor's misrule. For every Liberian who lost his or her life, many others were victims of robbery, rape, beatings, and other abuses. Even those fortunate enough to escape direct violence were subjected to constant fear and uncertainty. A nation that a generation ago had experienced the hope of real progress was thrown into a long dark night of chaos. Even the beginnings of recovery will be a difficult process, to be measured in years.

The Liberian Experience in Retrospect

If we examine the overall course of Liberian history, from the 1820s to the present day, we find that it has been shaped by cycles of progress and retrogression. The first of these cycles took place in the 19th century. The Americo-Liberians, strangers in their ancestral land, nevertheless succeeded in building a homeland for themselves. They adapted political institutions to their needs, and for a time had an active public life with relatively free and open elect ions. Liberian merchants established themselves as a dynamic element of the West African regional economy.

This progress, however, gave way to stagnation and decline in the later 19th century. The political system degenerated into one-party rule. Liberian traders, lacking the capital to adopt the new technology of steam, and unable to compete with Europeans supported by colonial governments, were driven out of markets where they had once been active. The Americo-Liberians, instead of providing a beacon of light to their tribal countrymen, reduced them into semi-servitude. The Firestone scandal and the near-loss of Liberian independence marked the low point of this first cycle.

Recovery began, however tentatively, during the long presidency of William V.S. Tubman. He began to institute long-needed reforms, even though he subsequently allowed them to stall. His efforts were, however, taken up with greater vigor by President William R. Tolbert.

The judgment of the 1970s and 1980s on the efforts of the Tolbert government was often a harsh one, as has been outlined previously in this document. There can be no doubt that President Tolbert shared many of the flaws of other African leaders of his generation. Beginning as a populist, who rode to his inauguration in a Volkswagen, he did tend over time to adopt many of the trappings of quasi-royalty. A produce of the old Americo-Liberian elites, and of a time when Africa invested too much hope in "Big Man" leaders, Tolbert was inevitably a victim of his background and his times.

Viewed in retrospect, however, from the perspective of the early 21st century, we may pass a more measured and balanced verdict on the leadership of President Tolbert. If the statues of himself that he placed in public squares seem foolish and egotistical, they still imposed only a tiny fraction of the burden on Liberia that the grandiose palaces of other African leaders of his time imposed on their countries. If his government often suffered from severe inefficiency and mismanagement, he nevertheless provided an environment in which schools and other independent institutions could grow. Given time, a new generation of Liberians, better-educated, would have been prepared to take their country forward.

Tragically, the potential of this generation – what we might not unfairly call the Tolbert generation – was almost entirely thrown away during the long slide toward chaos that followed President Tolbert's assassination in 1980.

IX. Conclusion

"The Love of Liberty Brought Us Here." That was the motto adopted by the Americo-Liberian settlers in the 19th century. It remains to this day, emblazoned proudly on Liberia's coat of arms. Yet, by failing to grant liberty to the Africans among whom they settled, in the end they also lost their own.

As early as 1887, the Americo-Liberians sacrificed their own domestic liberty, in the form of truly free elections, accepting the one-party dominance of the True Whig Party in order to present a united front against the indigenous people. The reforms of the Tubman and Tolbert eras, from 1944 to 1980, were too often flawed and incomplete, giving new hope to many Liberians, but causing expectations to rise faster than they could be met. The continuing frustrations of the indigenous population – and indeed of younger Americo-Liberians – finally boiled over in fury of the 1979 rice riots and the rejoicing that surrounded the 1980 coup by Samuel Doe. Since 1980, however, Liberia has experienced not liberation but only turmoil and destruction.

It is perhaps impossible to blame the early Americo-Liberian settlers for their choices. They were products of their time and culture. In an age of white imperialism, they slipped easily into the role of black imperialists. In doing so, however, they imposed a terrible burden on future Liberians, including their own children. For example, it was long-standing policy – as with European imperialists – to station "native" soldiers among tribes other than their own. This was done to minimize any sympathy between the soldiers and the populations they were used to control. It set the stage, however, for the emergence of violent tribal conflict during the Doe years and the civil war that followed. In this and many other ways, the Americo-Liberians failed to forge a nation when they had the opportunity to do so.

We cannot change the past, but we can act to change the future. One such action must be for the United States to take greater responsibility for the fate of a nation it helped bring into being, and that began as America's first overseas colony. The first stage in taking responsibility must in turn be to gain awareness of the problem. Liberia is a small, distant country, but it is one to which Americans have old and deep ties – yet ties of which most Americans are wholly unaware. It is the intent of this document to play some small part in this process of education and understanding.

References

Andrews, G. Henry (1993). *Cry, Liberia, Cry!* New York: Vantage Press.

Bright, Nancy Oku, Dir. (2002). Liberia: America's Stepchild. PBS Home Video.

Ciment, James (1998). The Idea of Liberia. *American Legacy* (Fall), pp. 33-42.

Drury, Bob; and Roston, Aram (2001). Pat Robertson's Gold Fever. *GQ* (December), pp. 229-235ff.

"Expectations High as Liberia's Next Leader Returns Home" (2003). *Los Angeles Times*, from Reuters (October 14), p. A10.

Jelinek, Pauline (2003). *Laredo Morning Times*, from AP (July 4), p. A13.

"Liberia's Fine Balance: All Hopes Hinge on Taylor Exile" (2003). Agence Presse-France (August 10). Via Clarinet

Dr. J. Mamadee Ghorpu-Dolo Woah-Tee, Sr.
<http://quickstart,clari.net/qs_se/webnews/wed/bq/Qliberia-taylor-handover.RwIY_DaA.html>

Liebenow, J. Gus (1987). *Liberia: The Quest for Democracy*. Bloomington: Indiana University Press.

Sawyer, Amos (1988). *Effective Immediately: Dictatorship in Liberia, 1890-1986: A Personal Perspective*. Cadiere en Keer, Netherlands: Africa Centre.

Taryor, Nya Kwiawon, Sr., ed. (1985). *Justice, Justice: A Cry of My People*. Chicago: Strugglers' Community Press.

Wise, Jacqui (2003). Aid Agencies Prepare to Tackle Desperate Situation in Liberia. *Bulletin of the World Health Organization* (81), p. 694.

The Presidents of Liberia

Joseph Jenkins Roberts	**Stephen Allen Benson**	**Daniel Bashiel Warner**	**James Spriggs Payne**
Born in Virginia, US	Born in Maryland, US	Born in US	Born in Virginia, US
Served: 1847-1856; 1872-1874	Served: 1856-1864	Served: 1864-1868	Served: 1868-1870; 1876-1878

Edward James Roye	**Anthony William Gardiner**	**Alfred Francis Russell**	**Hilary Richard W. Johnson**
Born in Ohio, US	Born in Maryland, US	Born in US	Born in Monrovia, Liberia
Served: 1870-1871	Served: 1878-1883	Served: 1883-1884 V.P. to Gardiner Completed Gardiner's term	Served: 1884-1892

**Joseph James
Cheeseman**
Born in US
Served: 1892-1896

**William David
Coleman**
Born in US
Served: 1896-1900

**Garretson W.
Gibson**
Born in US
Served: 1900-1904

Arthur Barclay
Born in Barbados
Served: 1904-1912

**Daniel Edward
Howard**
Born in Monrovia,
Liberia
Served: 1912-1920

**Charles Dunbar
Burgess King**
Born in Sierra
Leone
Served: 1920-1930

**Edwin James
Barclay**
Born in Monrovia,
Liberia
Served: 1930-
1944

**William V. S.
Tubman**
Born in Harper,
Liberia
Served: 1944-1971

**William Richard
Tolbert, Jr.**
Born in
Bensonville,
Liberia
Served: 1971-1980

**Samuel Kanyon
Doe**
Born in Tuzon,
Liberia
Served: 1980-
1990

**Charles M.
Ghankay Taylor**
Born in Artington,
Liberia
Served: 1997-2003

Moses Zeh Blah
Born in Toweh
Town, Liberia
Served: 2003

**Charles Gyude
Bryant**
Born in Liberia
Served: 2003-

These are photos of the past and present leaders of the Republic of Liberia since independence (1847-2004). With the exception of two (the late former Military ruler and later, President Samuel Kayan Doe, and Moses Zeh Blah) the rest are descendants of the settlers who landed on the shores of what is today called Liberia, in the early 1800s through the efforts of the American Colonization Society (A.C.S.). It is well to note that Liberia's history can be divided into three key categories; they can be broken down as follow:

- The first Republic: During this period, the settlers and their descendants ruled the country from Independence (1847)to April, 1980 and ended with the violent overthrow of the late William Richard Tolbert, the last Americo-Liberian President of that era. For 133 years, the descendants of the settlers ruled Liberia and during these years, most of the seeds that were sow began to germinate in the late 70s and 80s;

- The second Republic: This time, and through the influence of so-called change advocates (The U.P.P., P.A.L., MOJA, etc.), the Liberian people decided to experiment with Military rule and this took place from 1980 to 1989 under Samuel K. Doe. It was not only disappointing, embarrassing and disgraceful but most disastrous;

- Chaos and Anarchy permeated Liberia between December, 1989 to August, 2003 when Charles Taylor, along with his rebels, invaded Liberia on that Christmas eve; and

- The third Republic: This republic witnessed a failed attempt to convert a rebel group into a credible governing body. The entire World saw how this experiment came to an end under Charles Taylor. During this time, the United Nations put sanctions on Liberia and Mr. Taylor, the then sitting President, was indicted by an international court for bearing the greatest responsibility for war crimes and human rights violations.

Counties of Liberia

Maryland County
Karluway Dist., Pleebo
Dist., Barrobo Dist.,
Greater Harper Dist.

Grand Kru County
BarclayVille Dist., Buah
Dist., SassTown Dist.,
Trembo Dist., Garraway
Dist., Wedebbo Dist.

Grand Gedeh County
Gbarzon Dist., Tchien
Dist., Konobo Dist.

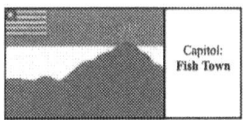

River Gee County
Webbo Dist., Gbeapo
Dist., Tienpo Dist.,
Potuopo Dist., Sarbo
Dist., Chedepo Dist.

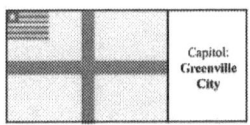

Sinoe County
Nyomopo Dist., Upper
Kpayan Dist., Lower
Kpayan Dist., Juarzon
Dist., GreenVille Dist.

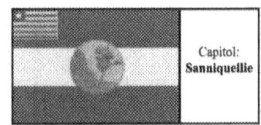

Nimba County
Bain-Yarpea Dist.,
Gbehlay-Gey Dist.,
Saclepea-Mah Dist., Tapita
Dist., Yarwin- Menhosonoh
Dist., Zoe-Geh Dist.,
Saniquellie

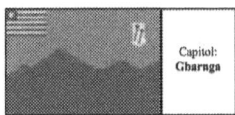

Bong County
Fuamah Dist., Kokoya
Dist., Sanoyea Dist.,
Panta Dist., Zota Dist.,
Suacoco Dist.,
Gbarnga Dist.

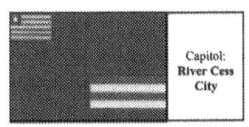

River Cess County
Central Rivercess Dist.,
Timbo Dist., Yamee Dist.

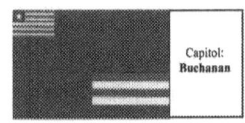

Grand Bassa County
No. One Dist., No. Two
Dist., No. Three Dist., No.
Four Dist., Buchanan Dist.

Lofa County
Zorzor Dist., Voinjama
Dist., Vahun Dist.,
Salayea Dist., Kolahun
Dist.

Gbarpolu County
Foya Dist., Belle Dist.,
Bokomu Dist., Bopolu
Dist., Gbarma Dist.

Bomi County
Mecca Swehn Dist.,
Diewioin Dist., Klay Dist.

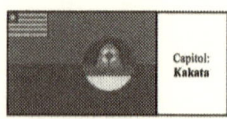

Margibi County
Gibi Dist., Marshall Dist.,
Kakata Dist.

Montserrado County
Careysburgh Dist., Todee
Dist., St. Paul River Right
Bank Dist., St. Paul River
Left Bank Dist., Greater
Monrovia Dist.

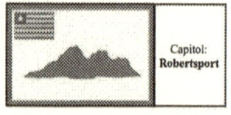

Cape Mt. County
Garwolo Dist., Gola
Koneh Dist., Lower Tewor
Dist., Upper Tewor Dist.,
Robertsport Dist.

Mrs. Cecelia Paye Woah-Tee has, and continues to be over the years, the most supportive, dedicated devoted, caring and loving wife any good man would want to be with for life. For all of the above, and moreover, her God-fearing nature, I salute and recognize her through this world-wide public medium.

Official Holidays of the United States and Liberia

LIBERIA	UNITED STATES
January 1st New Year's Day	January 1st: New Year's Day
February 11th Armed Forces Day	January, third Monday: Martin Luther, Jr. Day
February 14th: Literacy Day	January 20th, every fourth year following Presidential election: Inauguration Day
2nd Wednesday in March: Decoration Day	February, third Monday: Washington's Birthday/honors Washington, but also Lincoln and other past American Presidents as "Presidents' Day
March 15th: Joseph Jenkins Roberts Birthday	May, last Monday: Memorial Day
2nd Friday in April: Fast and Prayer Day	July 4th: Independence Day
April 15th: Africa Freedom Day	September, first Monday: Labor Day

Dr. J. Mamadee Ghorpu-Dolo Woah-Tee, Sr.

LIBERIA	UNITED STATES

LIBERIA

May 14th:
Unification Day

May 25th:
African Liberation Day

July 26th:
Independence Day

August 24th:
Flag Day

October 24th:
United Nations Day

1st Thursday in November:
Thanksgiving Day

November 29th:
William V.S. Tubman Birthday

December 10th:
Human Rights Day

December 25th:
Christmas

UNITED STATES

October, second Monday:
Columbus Day

November 11:
Veterans Day

November, fourth Thursday:
Thanksgiving

December 25:
Christmas